# AROUND THE GLOBE

# MUST SEE PLACES IN NORTH AMERICA

Speedy Publishing LLC
40 E. Main St. #1156
Newark, DE 19711
www.speedypublishing.com

North America is a continent wholly within the Northern Hemisphere and almost wholly within the Western Hemisphere. It can also be considered a northern subcontinent of the Americas. The heart of North America beats through towering forests, undulating fields, high-plain deserts, pulsating metropolises and offbeat oases.

Mount Assiniboine is a mountain located on the Great Divide, on the British Columbia/Alberta border in Canada. It is the highest peak in the Southern Continental Ranges of the Canadian Rockies. it is the highest peak in the Southern Continental Ranges of the Canadian Rockies.

The Wave is a geological marvel found on the slopes of the Coyote Buttes, at the Arizona-Utah border. It is famous among hikers and photographers for its colorful, undulating forms, and the rugged, trackless hike required to reach it. “The Wave” consists of intersecting U-shaped troughs that have been eroded into Navajo Sandstone of Jurassic age.

Lake Louise, named Lake of the Little Fishes by the Stoney Natoka First Nations people, is a glacial lake within Banff National Park in Alberta, Canada. The magnificent turquoise colour of the water is a result of the light filtering effect of rock flour in the glacial runoff, though you need to visit between late July and August to see the water at its brightest. Lake Louise is named after the Princess Louise Caroline Alberta (1848–1939), the fourth daughter of Queen Victoria and the wife of the Marquess of Lorne, who was the Governor General of Canada from 1878 to 1883.

Devils Tower is an igneous intrusion or laccolith in the Bear Lodge Mountains. Etched in uniform vertical ridges, the tower is a haven for rock climbers. The landscape surrounding Devils Tower is composed mostly of sedimentary rocks. The top of Devils Tower is approximately the size of a football field, though is slightly rocky and dome-shaped.

The Carlsbad Caverns are a series of natural limestone caves located in Carlsbad Caverns National Park, in the Guadalupe Mountains of New Mexico. Carlsbad Cavern includes a large cave chamber, the Big Room, a natural limestone chamber that is almost 4,000 feet long, 625 feet wide, and 255 feet high at the highest point. It is the fifth largest chamber in North America and the twenty-eighth largest in the world.

The Las Vegas Strip is a stretch of Las Vegas Boulevard South in Clark County, Nevada, internationally known for its concentration of resort hotels and casinos along its route. Many of the largest hotel, casino, and resort properties in the world are located on the Las Vegas Strip. Fifteen of the world's 25 largest hotels by room count are on the Strip, with a total of over 62,000 rooms. One of the most visible aspects of Las Vegas' cityscape is its use of dramatic architecture.

Central Park is an urban park in the central part of the borough of Manhattan, New York City. Today, Central Park is the most visited urban park in the United States as well as one of the most filmed locations in the world. A total of 29 sculptures by sculptors such as Augustus Saint-Gaudens, Emma Stebbins, and John Quincy Adams Ward have been erected over the years, most donated by individuals or organizations. Much of the first statuary placed was of authors and poets, in an area now known as Literary Walk.

Times Square is a major commercial intersection and neighborhood in Midtown Manhattan, New York City. Brightly adorned with billboards and advertisements, Times Square is sometimes referred to as The Crossroads of the World, The Center of the Universe, and the heart of The Great White Way. Times Square is one of the world's most visited tourist attractions. Times Square has been featured countless times in literature, on television, in films, in video games, and in music videos.

www.LG.co
Corona
Light
Coca-Cola
NEW THINKING.
"THE
DISNEY
swatch

Monument Valley is a region of the Colorado Plateau characterized by a cluster of vast sandstone buttes, the largest reaching 1,000 ft above the valley floor. Monument Valley experiences a desert climate with cold winters and hot summers. While the summers may be hot, the heat is tempered by region's aridity and high altitude. Monument Valley has been featured in many forms of media since the 1930s.

Mount Rushmore National Memorial is a sculpture carved into the granite face of Mount Rushmore near Keystone, South Dakota, in the United States. Mount Rushmore is largely composed of granite. Mount Rushmore has become an iconic symbol of the United States, and has appeared in works of fiction, and has been discussed or depicted in other popular works. It attracts over two million people annually.

Calakmul is a Maya archaeological site in the Mexican state of Campeche, deep in the jungles of the greater Petén Basin region. Calakmul was one of the largest and most powerful ancient cities ever uncovered in the Maya lowlands. Calakmul was a major Maya power within the northern Petén region of the Yucatán of southern Mexico. There are 6,750 ancient structures identified at Calakmul; the largest of which is the great pyramid at the site.

Chichen Itza as a large pre-Columbian city built by the Maya people of the Terminal Classic period. The archaeological site is located in Tinum Municipality, Yucatán State, Mexico. Chichen Itza was one of the largest Maya cities and it was likely to have been one of the mythical great cities. Chichen Itza is one of the most visited archaeological sites in Mexico; an estimated 1.2 million tourists visit the ruins every year.

Watkins Glen State Park is located outside the village of Watkins Glen, New York, south of Seneca Lake in Schuyler County in the Finger Lakes region. The park has comfortable camping sites, as well as picnic tables and pavilions, food, playground, pool, showers, recreation programs, tent and trailer sites, fishing, hunting, hiking and cross-county skiing. The centerpiece of the 1000-acre park is a 400-foot-deep narrow gorge cut through rock by a stream.

The Mauna Kea Observatories are an independent collection of astronomical research facilities located on the summit of Mauna Kea on the Big Island of Hawai'i, USA. An adjacent visitor information station is located at 9,200 feet. The summit of Mauna Kea is so high that tourists are advised to stop at the visitor station for at least 30 minutes to acclimate to atmospheric conditions before continuing to the summit.

Mammoth Hot Springs is a large complex of hot springs on a hill of travertine in Yellowstone National Park adjacent to Fort Yellowstone and the Mammoth Hot Springs Historic District. This area has been thermally active for several thousand years. The Mammoth area exhibits much evidence of glacial activity from the Pinedale Glaciation.

Banff National Park is Canada's oldest national park, established in 1885. Banff National Park is located in the Rocky Mountains on Alberta's western border with British Columbia in the Alberta Mountain forests ecoregion. The main commercial centre of the park is the town of Banff, in the Bow River valley. Banff National Park is the most visited Alberta tourist destination and one of the most visited national parks in North America.

Johnston Creek is a tributary of the Bow River in Canada's Rocky Mountains. The creek is located in Banff National Park. As Johnston Creek approaches the Bow River, it flows through a large canyon formed by erosion over thousands of years. The creek has cut through the limestone rock to form sheer canyon walls, as well as waterfalls, tunnels, and pools. Ice climbing is a popular activity on the frozen waterfalls in winter.

Avalanche Lake is located in Glacier National Park, in the U. S. state of Montana. Avalanche Lake is southwest of Bearhat Mountain and receives meltwater from Sperry Glacier. After a 2-hour hike among the peaks and valleys of Montana's Glacier National Park, lucky travelers will arrive at Avalanche Lake, an unbelievably clear lake nestled among snowy mountains and cascading waterfalls.

Custer State Park is a state park and wildlife reserve in the Black Hills of southwestern South Dakota, USA. The park is South Dakota's largest and first state park. Custer State Park has a natural bounty that rivals that of any national park in the West. The park is home to a famous herd of 1500 free roaming bison. Elk, mule deer, white tailed deer, mountain goats, bighorn sheep, pronghorn, mountain lions, and feral burros also inhabit the park.

Antelope Canyon is a slot canyon in the American Southwest. It is located on Navajo land east of Page, Arizona. Antelope Canyon was formed by erosion of Navajo Sandstone, primarily due to flash flooding and secondarily due to other sub-aerial processes. Antelope Canyon is a popular location for photographers and sightseers. Photography within the canyons is difficult due to the wide exposure range (often 10 EV or more) made by light reflecting off the canyon walls.

Crowsnest Pass is a high mountain pass across the Continental Divide of the Canadian Rockies on the Alberta/British Columbia border. Crowsnest Pass comprises a valley running east-west through Crowsnest Ridge. Crowsnest Pass is one of the most beautiful stops along Canada's Continental Divide. The Crowsnest Pass is the richest archaeological zone in the Canadian Rockies.

Horseshoe Bend is a horseshoe-shaped meander of the Colorado River located near the town of Page, Arizona, in the United States. It is so named by the shape of the meandering Colorado River below as it flows one way and then makes a quick "horseshoe" turn as it continues on its path through Lees Ferry and its journey through the Grand Canyon. The rock walls of Horseshoe Bend contain a variety of minerals, among which are hematite, platinum and garnet.

Canyonlands National Park is a U.S. National Park located in southeastern Utah near the town of Moab. Canyonlands National Park is an authentic playground of rivers, canyons, mesas, and arches. Canyonlands is a popular recreational destination. The geography of the park is well suited to a number of different recreational uses. Hikers, mountain bikers, backpackers, and four-wheelers all enjoy traveling the rugged, remote trails within the Park.

www.ingramcontent.com/pod-product-compliance
Lightning Source LLC
LaVergne TN
LVHW060830170826
845678LV00010B/1938

* 9 7 9 8 8 6 9 4 5 3 5 7 0 *